NOAH'S ARK

By Barbara Shook Hazen and Diane Muldrow

Illustrated by Mircea Catusanu

A GOLDEN BOOK • NEW YORK

ISBN: 978-0-375 84051-7
www.goldenbooks.com
Printed in China
10 9 8 7 6 5 4 3 2 1

Long ago, when the world was new, there lived a man named Noah.

Noah lived in peace and happiness with his family. God saw this and was pleased. God also saw that other people were selfish and cruel to each other.

God said to Noah, "I am going to wash away the evil in the world with a great flood." He told Noah to build a special boat, called an ark, to save his family.

"Bring into the ark two of every kind of animal," God told Noah. "Gather plenty of food and store it on the ark for everyone."

Noah told his family what God had said to him. "We must obey God," said Noah.

Noah and his family began their work right away. Some people laughed when they saw Noah building a big boat so far away from water. But Noah trusted God.

Noah's family gathered lots of food to take on the ark—berries, fruits, vegetables, nuts. They stored hay for the horses, grain for the cattle, and meat for the lions and tigers.

Finally, the ark was ready! That's when God sent Noah two of every kind of animal in the world.

In marched the animals, two by two,
The long-necked giraffe and the kangaroo,
The walrus and the wallaby, too—
Up the ramp, two by two.
Up the ramp flipped two slippery seals,
And after them came two electric eels,
Badger and beaver, bear and gnu—
Up the ramp, two by two.

After Noah's family and the last pair of animals had stepped into the ark, the Lord shut them in. Some raindrops fell, *plink-plunk,* on the roof of the ark.

It began to rain harder, and then it poured!
The wind howled. The thunder roared.
Lightning flashed in jagged streaks across
the sky.

Soon the ark began to float, and the water kept rising. After a while, even the mountain peaks disappeared from sight! It would rain for forty days and forty nights.

All life on earth was destroyed, but everyone in the ark was safe.

Noah and his family kept busy taking care of all the animals.

The animals grew uneasy. The wolves howled and the horses whinnied. Even the great striped tigers crouched in a corner and meowed like kittens.

Noah's family grew restless in the crowded, noisy ark. Had God forgotten them? Would it ever stop raining? But Noah trusted God. And finally, just as God had said it would, the rain stopped.

God made the sun shine
and a warm wind blow.
Little by little, the water
went down.

One day, the ark lurched
and bumped against the
top of a mountain.

Noah wanted to know if there was dry land anywhere. He sent a raven out a window. Away it flew, up into the sunny sky. But soon it came back. There had been no place for it to land.

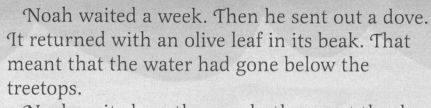

Noah waited a week. Then he sent out a dove. It returned with an olive leaf in its beak. That meant that the water had gone below the treetops.

Noah waited another week, then sent the dove out again. This time, the dove did not come back. That meant that the land was dry now, and the dove had found a place to live.

"Come out of the ark," God told Noah.

So Noah opened the door of the ark.
Fresh air rushed in. The people and the
animals felt warm sunlight on their faces.

The animals were so happy to be free! They pranced and hopped and waddled and slithered down the ramp onto dry land.

The bears ambled into the forests. The lions raced to the plains. The birds and monkeys hurried to the jungles. And some animals, the tame ones like the sheep and cattle, stayed close to Noah.

Noah's family was happy, too. They built an altar to God, and thanked God for keeping them safe. That's when God made a beautiful rainbow shine across the sky.

And God blessed Noah and his family, saying, "I will never again cover the earth with water. This rainbow is a sign of my promise to you. Whenever you see a rainbow, remember this promise."